ISBN 978-1-332-87480-4
PIBN 10293792

English
Français
Deutsche
Italiano
Español
Português

www.forgottenbooks.com

Mythology Photography **Fiction**
Fishing Christianity **Art** Cooking
Essays Buddhism Freemasonry
Medicine **Biology** Music **Ancient
Egypt** Evolution Carpentry Physics
Dance Geology **Mathematics** Fitness
Shakespeare **Folklore** Yoga Marketing
Confidence Immortality Biographies
Poetry **Psychology** Witchcraft
Electronics Chemistry History **Law**
Accounting **Philosophy** Anthropology
Alchemy Drama Quantum Mechanics
Atheism Sexual Health **Ancient History**
Entrepreneurship Languages Sport
Paleontology Needlework Islam
Metaphysics Investment Archaeology
Parenting Statistics Criminology
Motivational

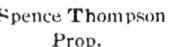

THE
LIBERTY BELL

NAVY YARD, PUGET SOUND   -   -   **NOVEMBER 1911**

VOL. VII   :   :   :   **NUMBER 9**

THE U. S. S. OREGON
THE BULL DOG OF THE NAVY

Y THE ACT OF JUNE 30, 1890, Congress provided for the first real battleship of this country. It is said that when the bill had been signed, the Secretary of the Navy, Benjamin F. Tracy sent for Lieutenant Lewis Nixon, then in the Constructor's Bureau and said to him informally: "Now sir, what you've to do is to design a ship that can lick anything afloat."

And Lieutenant Nixon designed the Oregon, the most powerful ship of her time. Two 13-inch guns were placed in each of two main turrets located over the keel fore and aft. One turret was then located on each quarter and two 8-inch guns mounted therein. Along the side armor walls were placed four 6-inch guns. She was equipped with twelve 3-inch for torpedo defense.

When completed, the ship that looks so small in these days of dreadnaughts and super dreadnaughts, made a very imposing sight and was reckoned by naval authorities to be par-excellence in battleship construction. The ship displaced nearly 10300 tons and the speed attained was 15,547 knots. Her armor varied from fifteen to eighteen inches in thickness.

Now we have much speedier ships of more than twice

her tonnage and steaming radius, and while she is over-shadowed by her more powerful sisters of recent date, it is well to remember that the Oregon showed the people and Congress that battleships could be built cheaper and better in this country than in Europe. She was the first of a series of ships to follow that have made the American Navy feared and respected in every quarter of the globe. So we can look on the Oregon as the cornerstone of the modern American Navy.

Designed as she was for a coast defense ship, yet she proved that in an emergency she was capable of carry-ing the war into the enemy's country.

On Tuesday, July the 7th, 1896, the builders, The Union Iron Works of San Francisco, turned her over to the Government of the United States and she was accepted at 11:45 a. m., by Lieutenant E. M. Hughes, U. S. N., on behalf of Rear Admiral Kirkland, commandant of the Mare Island Navy Yard. One week and one day later, almost to the hour on Wednesday, July 15, she went into commission, with Captain Henry L. Howison, commanding; Lieutenant Commander F. J. Drake, executive officer, and Lieutenant E. M. Hughes, navigator.

When the Secretary of the Navy, John D. Long, made his report, dated November 15, 1897, a few months before the war with Spain, the Oregon, Massachusetts, Indiana and Iowa, comprised the battleship fleet of our navy.

On March the 19th, 1898, she started on her memorable cruise from San Francisco to Key West, with Captain Clark commanding. Much has been said and written about that cruise, and indeed it was a remarkable per-formance for a "coast defense" vessel. The men in the "black gang" seem to have suffered most on this journey, on account of the poor ventilation in her fire rooms. Men in her fire rooms today say they have never experienced a hotter temperature anywhere than when steaming along at twelve knots.

Indeed it is said that at the battle of Santiago, when the Colon was fleeing from the Oregon and Brooklyn, with the slower Texas astern, Chief Engineer Milligan went into the suffocating stokehold to personally cheer and enthuse the exhausted men who were gasping for breath but keeping steam up until a speed of perhaps eighteen knots was attained. And this on a vessel that only made 15.547 knots on her trial trip! Of such men is the American Navy composed. It was then that the impatient younger officers on deck asked Captain Clark to let them try a shot and the Captain consented. The Chief Engineer came on deck black with coal dust to thank the Captain and say that his men were fainting below, but if they could hear a shot now and then they could live through and keep her going!

During the war with Spain the Oregon demonstrated her right to the sobriquet of "Bull Dog" a familiar title, by which she has been known ever since.

> "Bull Dog of the Navy, hail!
> Again we greet you on the sea;
> Old ship that weathered rock and gale
> Old ship that sought an enemy.
> Aye, sought and found, and on the quest
> Ten thousand miles of ocean swept:
> And, thundering round from out the West,
> A message from your muzzles leapt-
> A message we had counted on,
> And you delivered, Oregon.   —OUR NAVY.

The Oregon demonstrated her sea-worthiness on the cruise around the Horn, but if any further proof is needed, her behavior in a typhoon in 1902 is conclusive. She was enroute to Yokohama to join the Asiatic fleet under the command of Rear Admiral Evans. The typhoon struck her at midnight. One enormous sea swept over the entire ship, crushing in the starboard pilot house. But good seamanship on a good ship brought her through it with no further damage. She escaped with a sound hull and was later repaired in a Japanese ship yard.

The following officers have been in command of the Oregon from date of commission:

Captain H. L. Howison..............................1896-'97
Captain Chas. E. Clark............................1897-'98
Captain A. S. Barker...............................1898-'99
Captain G. F. F. Wilde............................1899-1901
Captain Chas. M. Thomas......................1901-'02
Captain J. G. Eaton.................................1902-'03
Captain Wm. F. Burwell.........................1903-'04
Captain John P. Merrill..........................1904-'06
Captain Chas. F. Pond............................1911

The Re=commissioning of the Oregon, August 29, 1911

In looking through the rough log of the Oregon's earlier history one is impressed with the severe punishments meted out for petty offenses. John Doe, on April 16th, 1897, was sentenced to five days B. & W. for late hammocks. Richard Roe got the same dose for smoking out of hours, and a summary court martial sentenced another offender to "3 & 30" for shirking duty. Nearly every day there was a mast report as long as your arm, many of them petty offences, and "B. & W." seemed to be the popular punishment, while restriction of shore liberty from three to six months was also often given as punishment. Thus we see how times have changed.

The West coast newspapers are devoting lots of space to the recommissioning of the Oregon which shows that the grand old ship has not been forgotten by the American public. An effort is being made to have the Oregon the first ship to pass through the Panama Canal upon its completion in 1915 as a mark of honor. President Taft has been quoted as saying he would do every thing in his power to further this plan. The Oregon has had a glorious and useful career and this crowning achievement, if carried out, will wind up a history that any ship may be proud of.

That our shipmates who were chosen to take the Oregon south on her latest cruise were proud of their ship is evidenced by the rapidity with which they procured Oregon cap ribbons to replace their old Pennsylvania ribbons.

Now that the championship series is over, maybe we can find a little real war news from China in the papers.

Most beautiful scenery in the world on the C. M. & P. S. Ry.

Captain Chas. F. Pond, U. S. N.

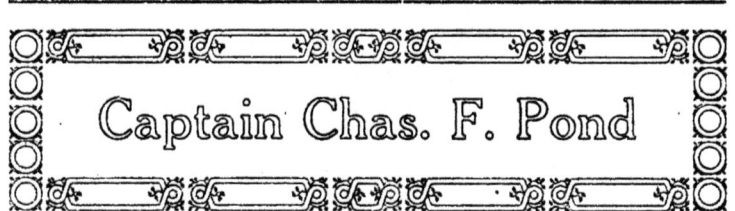

Captain Chas. F. Pond

Captain Chas F. Pond, commanding the Pacific Reserve Squadron, comprising at present the battleship Oregon, armored cruiser Pennsylvania, protected cruiser St. Louis and the torpedo boats Fox and Davis, was born in Brooklyn, Windham county, Connecticut, on October the 26th, 1856. He entered the Naval Academy as a cadet Midshipman, June 13, 1872, and graduated therefrom in 1876. His first sea duty was on the U. S. S. Pensacola, flag ship, U. S. S. Lackawanna and U. S. S. Tuscorera, Pacific station and California State Training Ship Jamestown.

In 1879 he was promoted to Ensign, and until 1883 served on U. S. Coast and Geodetic Survey steamer "Hassler," surveying coasts of California and Alaska and making magnetic survey of coast and islands from San Salvador to Sitka, Alaska. In 1883 he was engaged in the Hydrographic office, Washington, D. C. In 1884-5 he served on the U. S. S. Hartford, flagship, and the U. S. S. Wachusett, Pacific station.

In 1885 he was promoted to Lieutenant (J. G.) and was assigned to the Naval Observatory, Mare Island, where he remained until 1887, serving four months on the "Hassler" in '86, surveying coast of California. From 1887-90 served on the U. S. S. Ranger, surveying the coast of lower California. From 1891-94 was in charge of the Naval Observatory, Mare Island, Cal., having been promoted to Lieutenant. From '94 to '97 was attached to U. S. S. Alert, Pacific station, as navigator and senior watch officer, in summer of 1894 on Bering Sea patrol.

In 1897 he was assigned as Assistant Inspector of Ordinance, Navy Yard, New York. At the breaking out of the war with Spain he put the Collier Lebanon into commission at Boston, and from April to October served as Navigator on the U. S. S. Panther with Rear Admiral Sampson's fleet on north coast of Cuba in search of Cevera's fleet. After that fleet was located at Santiago, Cuba,

Seventy hours Seattle to Chicago via C. M. & P. S.

transported marines to Guantanamo and took part in the three days fighting there. After the capitulation of Santiago, he transported troops to Montauk Point.

From 1898 to 1902 he commanded the U. S. S. Iroquois, station ship at Honolulu, Hawaiian Islands. In 1901 he made a survey of the Midway Islands for cable station. While temporarily in command of the naval station, Honolulu, he located and made reservation of Naval Station, Pearl Harbor, and assisted the U. S. District Attorney in passing condemnation proceeding through the U. S. District Court and the U. S. Court of Appeals, San Francisco, Cal., securing for $100,000 land leasehold interests valued at over $1,000,000. In 1899 he was promoted to Lieutenant Commander.

In 1902 he went to the Naval Training Station, San Francisco, Cal., remaining until 1904. In 1903 he superintended for the Government the landing of the Pacific cable at the Midway Islands. In 1904-5 he commanded the U. S. S. Supply, station ship at Guam. In 1905 he was promoted to Commander, and assigned to the Navy Yard, Mare Island, as aid to the Commandant and Inspector of Ordnance in charge of Naval Magazine at that station. In the winter of 1905-6 he commanded the U. S. S. Lawton on a record speed trip to Cavite and return.

In 1907 he assumed command of the U. S. S. Buffalo and proceeded north on the Bering Sea patrol, then located and reserved naval coaling station of 3150 acres on Resurrection Bay, Alaska, which when the Matanuska coal fields are opened up, will undoubtedly be the source of fuel supply for the Navy in the Pacific Ocean.

He was Light House Inspector of the 13th district, Portland, Ore., during the years 1908-9, and while so serving recommended over 150 additional aids to navigation in Alaskan waters, many of which have since been established.

In 1909 he was promoted to Captain and in July assumed command of the U. S. S. Pennsylvania, which position he has held to date.

The Pennsylvania entered dry dock October 17. We still linger, and from present appearances are due to stay a couple of weeks yet.

Dogs

When one of our new ships went into commission the crew got their heads together and decided that the ship must have a mascot. Dogs, cats, goats etc., were recommended, but still they could not agree which one to choose. Finally it decided to consult old Billy Thompson, the ships quarter-master, who could tell about mascots etc., as far back as '61.

The committee on mascots marched in a body to Billy's quarters and explained the situation to him.

Leisurely lighting his pipe, Billy said: "Maties, they dont put a ship like this wun inter commishun every day, an' a ship widout er mascot is like er sailor wid er pipe an, no. terbaccer.

"Now speakin' 'bout dorgs, I'm well 'sperienced wid 'em. I've bin sick, bited, and even been put in the Pie wagon over 'em. There's enuff dorgs aboard ship without gettin' any more. Now, we often has dorgs (sausages) fer breakfast, doors an' hatches has dorgs on 'em (clamps used for securing), then there's the dorg watch (a shift of watches to change the hours), an' wunce I got ther pie wagon fer fetchin a live dorg orf (a full bottle of liquor), and dog gast it I got thutty days fer it.

"We's dont need no dorg. They sez er dead borg tells no talea, so anything but er dorg will fill ther billet.

Herman Ebeneezer, who had overheard the consultation remarked to the committee on mascots: ',I'll be dog gurnelled if I dont send for Dad's mooley calf, if youse fellers will pay the freight."

P. S. - - The mooley calf arrived O. K. but met its fate in the Galley.

—From Man-o-war Yarns in
THE AMERICAN BATTLESHIP IN COMMISSION.

"Van" is the Blue Jacket's friend.

PAID OFF

(CONTINUED FROM LAST MONTH)

At just five minutes to eight o'clock John entered the railroad offices and reported to the head clerk in charge. "Ah, lets see, what is your name?" he asked John, and on being informed, made a rumbling noise in his throat that reminded John of his former skipper, when he had a man before him at the mast. In fact he was almost prepared to hear "deck court," but instead was told where to report to work.

John found his fellow workman very accommodating and pleasant fellows to get along with, and it was only a matter of a few hours until he had mastered the details of his job and was getting along fine. He found that his work was not hard, but demanded a close attention to detail and mistakes were not tolerated. When a batch of bills left his hands they went to another man higher up for verification, so he learned to be very careful.

As the days went by John learned many things about life in the civil world, things that he had not dreamed of before. For instance he had supposed that discipline was an unknown factor outside the military service, but he was beginning to see that discipline existed everywhere. Whenever the General Freight Agent made his appearance in the office there was quite a flurry and buzz of excitement and turning of heads to get a sight of the great man. John compared him to an Admiral and came to the conclusion that the service was not the only place where an exalted position rates attention. Even the head clerk was quite an important personage and when he spoke to any one that person moved with alacrity. Everything went to show that in any walk of life the boss man was It, whether he wore gold lace in a military service, or Dungarees on a contract job.

John had worked in his new position about two weeks before anything hapepned to get him "in bad." The alarm clock which he had purchased, failed to awaken him one morning and when he did wake up he saw to his horror that it was nearly nine o'clock. Hastily dressing he set out for the office, stopping at a little lunch counter barely long enough for a cup of coffee.

"I wonder what they do to a fellow for being overtime," he mused, and he remembered seeing a card over the chief clerk's desk that said something about promptness being the chief virtue.

Not knowing what was in store for him he felt a little nervous and when he reached the office and went in to report to the chief clerk he was conscious of an uncomfortable feeling in his chest, and found himself continually throwing back his shoulders as though to rid himself of this feeling.

"And what is the matter with you this morning, Mr. Carter, if I may ask," his chief asked him. So John told him about the defective clock. The chief listened until he had finished, then delivered himself of the following:

"Mr. Carter, this company, and I might add, no other company, will long tolerate a man who comes late to his work. In the first place it denotes unreliability, something we have no use for in our employees. In the second place, the company pays you for full eight hours of your time every day, and when you come late they are paying for something they do not get. That is all; don't let it happen again."

John walked away feeling slightly relieved, and it must be confesesd, a little hot under the collar. "Gee," said he to himself, "that was some bawling out for just an hour and a half late." But that evening he bought a new aalrm clock.

One Sunday John took a car out to a park on a hill overlooking the city. One of his fellow workmen had told him that a beautiful view of the city could be obtained there. He found that the attractions of the place had not been exaggerated in the slightest. The city lay stretched at his feet, almost every detail showing in the clear mountain air. To the south of the city lay the harbor, filled with shipping and—what was that long "war-colored" ship with military mast? As he lived, it was his old ship, at anchor in the bay. When did she arrive, he wondered. She had gone north again shortly after he had been discharged. Some of his former shipmates might be in the city now. He would go back to town and lock them up, and failing to find them he would go aboard in the afternoon.

But his eyes were attracted to the old ship again. Didn't she look graceful with her tall funnels in perfect alignment, the sun glinting on the black muzzles of her turret guns? Every line and curve and angle bespoke speed and power. Her sombre coat of "war-color" added a touch of grimness to the picture that was slightly relieved by the brightness of the bit of bunting on her flagstaff astern, the Colors. · John unconsciously removed his cap and drew a deep breath, his eyes glistening from some emotion it would have been hard for him to describe.

A wave of some feeling, something like homesickness swept over him. Long he looked and steady. He could see white clad figures moving about on her decks looking like pygmies in the distance.

Suddenly from afar came the silvery tones of a bugle. He listened intently, marveling meanwhile that he had never before noticed the exquisite beauty of the bugle notes. They were calling away the second steamer.

He watched the steamer cast loose from the boom and describing a perfect arc, approach the gangway. He turned away, conscious of a peculiar gnawing feeling in his breast. "Why," he asked himself, "should he be so affected by such a commonplace scene, a scene he had witnessed hundreds of times at colse quarters?" ·

The answer came with sickening force. He was lonesome. He wanted to go back. He wanted to be back among his old shipmates, among old familiar scenes. The freedom of the outside was losing its attraction. Immediately he began conjuring up a dozen reasons why he should not go back. He had a good position, and while promotion was not as rapid as he had expected, still it would come some day. His work was pleasant and hours comparatively short and after working hours he was his own boss. He tried to recall the feeling he had had in the South Sea Islands that time when for 48 hours at a stretch he had shoveled coal, an hour on and an hour off— a time when the thermometer had registered 115 in the hold of the collier and the dust was so thick it could almost be shoveled out. But it was no go. This picture, vivid enough at the time, failed to cause even a grimmace now.

All he could see was that calm stately ship with the beautiful lines riding peacefully at her anchor there in the harbor.

His mind was made up. Tomorrow he would quit his job and go back in the service, among his kind, to live his kind of life.

Did he live to regret his decision? Ask any second cruise man. John is only an imaginary person and can't tell us. But the moral: "Go Inland."

CUT IT REGULATION BY GOLLY!

We have some girls on this old ship,
Who wouldn't sign up for a barber slip,
But some one put the First Luff hip;
And, they cut it regulation. By Golly!
Both far and near the word was passed
"Get that hair trimmed or you'll be classed
When gum boot takes you to the mast."
And, "Cut it regulation. By Golly."
Montie stood by his red plush chair,
Runnin' his fingers through auburn hair,
When a bull-like voice rang thro' the air.
"Cut it regulation. By Golly."
He smiled a smile and the clippers whirls,
As he clipped the hair of the sea goin' girls,
And they looked like h—l without their curls.
'Twas cut regulation, By Golly!
As they all lined up at the port gangway,
To go ashore on the liberty day,
You could hear each one say,
'Twas cut regulation, By Golly!"
But my short "butt" will soon roll 'round
Then no more will they clip my crown.
I'll let 'er go till she grows righ down
To my waist, By Golly!

—Jayhawker.

Mr. B. F. B. Wright, once professor of chemistry at Harvard, has perfected a powder that he claims to be three times as powerful as dynamite and cannot be accidentally exploded. He states that its use on warships would prevent the damage done by the recoil of the large guns and would prolong the life of the weapons.

When the staff cartoonist casually remarked the other day in the presence of the office devil that he had drawn a series of pictures for one of our large service publications which he had called dreams, the devil straightway had an inspiration of which the following sample is the awful result:

DREAMS.

Wunce I had a dream,
A layin' on a chest,
'Twas awful hot an' I wus tired,
An' I dreamed my very best.
I didn't dream of bein' an Admiral,
Like sailors generally does,
Nor did I dream of war an' glory
Nor liberty an' mess gear like alwus
Comes to sailors, they say. No sir,
Not I, by gum! I dreamed, an' gosh 'twas
That I wus a seaman on Paw's ranch!
I had the 12 to 2 on the starboard bridge,
Down in the pasture, across the branch;
An' Paw, he had the Deck,
An' he sure wus rarin' 'round
'Caus the ace of spades wus missin'
An' the frost wus hard aground!

The "Milwaukee" is the New Steel Trail.

An' he roars, roars he, "Messenger!"
I jumped like I wus shot, an' none too soon
"Messenger, bring the rabbit piece,
"I'll have to shoot the moon!
"For we're in uncharted seas,
"An' our reckonin's dead, I guess.
"An I hear the breakers a breakin'
"Up our fall pasture by gum! An', yes
"I hear the ringin' of the bell
Made fast to old "Black Bess,"
A warnin' all good sailors that milkin' time
Is here. An' the wind is roarin' in the west
Lot through the maples.
Hark! at that dread sound the helmsman
Threw the wheel clear over the barn;
The skipper ('twas ma) came runnin'
To learn what wus the alarm.
An' Paw, he cries, cries he, "We're lost, sir!
Shiver my timbers, by gum, there's no hope,
Our starboard binnacle's afoul the binder
An' our yearlin' colts are broke.
An' the trackless fields are one wild mass
Of weeds an' thistles an' snares,
An' the wires are down 'round the oatfield green,
An' the field is full of tares.
Oh! save the ship, the captain cried,
Then came an awful sound—
A roarin' from the chicken-room hatch
Where the Plymouth Rocks abound.
'Tis the incubator, gone by the board,
And the wail of the new-born chicks
Could be plainly heard above the rustling
Hay in the cattle rleks;
And the smell of flapjacks burnin'
Filled the frosty air,
And all around wus wreck an' carnage,
An' confusion everywhere.
An' when it seemed that all wus lost,
The bridge, the fields, an' all the rest,
I woke with a pain In my starboard side,
From sleepin' on a chest!

                              BY DUFF—
            (With abject appologies to our readers)

THE LIBERTY BELL
PRINTED AND PUBLISHED ON BOARD THE
U. S. S. PENNSYLVANIA

Published on the fifth of every month in the interests of the service in general, and the U. S. S. Pennsylvania and her officers and crew in particular.

Single copies, 15c. $1.50 per year. 75c for six months
Advertising rates on Application.

A. J. McDaniel, Printer, U. S. N. ....Editor
George Heller, Yeoman 3rd class, U. S. N. ....Sporting Editor
W. H. McDaniel, H. App. U. S. N. ....•.........Manager

To "put a ship in commission" does not mean much to the average lay mind. But to those upon whom the actual work falls the task becomes one of gigantic proportions, necessitating long hours of extra labor for men who already have their hands full.

In the first place the store rooms of the ship are to be filled with provisions sufficient to last anywhere from three to ten months. All her equipment must be moved from the yard storerooms to the storerooms aboard ship. On the G. S. K. force falls the lot of taking care of this gear, enumerating it, putting it on the books under the proper titles and accounting for every little screw and nut. Men are working every day putting stores and equipment aboard. Then the ship's empty bunkers must be filled with coal. When she is coaled and equipped and provisioned and ready to have her crew assigned then the ship's writer and Master-at-Arms begin to take off their coats and go to work. Every man who comes aboard must have a certain billet, designated by a number which assigns him his division, section and watch. He must have a certain place to swing and stow his hammock, a certain place to eat, a certain cleaning station, etc. The ship's writer puts all this on the books and to the Chief Master-at-Arms falls the job of actually billeting and messing the ship. As near as possible he must get billets for a division in the same part of the ship. The messes must also be arranged in like manner. The ship has been equipped with enough tables and benches to accommodate the crew. The messes are laid out from No. 1 up, odd numbers on

the starboard side, even numbers on the port side. All
the mess gear used by each man must be drawn from
the General Store Keeper of the ship and signed for by
the Chief Master-at-Arms. Then each messman draws a
full set for each man on his mess and signs for the same.
All this means lots of book work for the G. S. K. yeoman,
for every little article drawn has to be entered on the
books and accounted for.

While all this is going on the heads of the various
departments are having the time of their lives assigning
their men to the various stations in their departments. In
the Engineers department watch bills must be made out,
men assigned to the various auxiliary machinery, such as
ice machine, steering engine room, dynamo room, and
mess cooks and compartment cleaners must be detailed.
Every man must be assigned his cleaning station as in
the deck force.

In the Ordnance department gunner's mates and their
strikers must be detailed for every gun, magazines must
be inspected and powder tested and in fact every department on the ship is very busy.

Of course some confusion is bound to exist for a few
days, but thanks to discipline and system, things are
working smoothly before many days.

Chief Yeoman Baylor and Ship's Cook Bugman are
demonstrating what can be done in the way of feeding a
ship's company the "way mother used to." A little heat
goes a long ways towards making grub palatable. Keep
up the good work, fellows. And if you could only devise
some way to heat up those cold stone dishes it would
help some more, wouldn't it?

Many may be surprised that we should publish this
month, and indeed we are a little surprised ourselves, to
see the book actually in print. It has been a hard month
for ye editor. What four men did formerly, we have
done all by our lonesome this month, and if we can't be
proud of the result, we are at least proud of the effort.

**Take your homeward bounder on the Best Road—The
Milwaukee.**

NAVY YARD NOTES.

The monitor Cheyenne and navy yard tug Pawtucket were placed in drydock October 11, for periodic docking and repairs.

The protected cruiser St. Louis, has been ordered to take the place of the old wooden ship Pensacola as receiving ship at the Naval Training Station at Yerba Beuna, Cal., in San Francisco bay. Word was received from the navy department to get the St. Louis in readiness for the cruise to San Francisco as soon as practicable.

The St. Louis was several months ago under orders to succeed the old wooden receiving ship Independence at the Mare Island yards, but on assignment of the St. Louis to the Pacific reserve fleet, the St. Louis' former orders were annulled.

The assignment of the St. Louis to the San Francisco training station is following out the policy announced by the navy department of abolishing the use of wooden vessels as receiving ships.

Assistant Paymaster W. R. Van Buren has been transferred from the Mare Island Navy Yard to duty as assistant to the general storekeeper of this yard.

Commander Kuenzli, U. S. N., reported for duty Saturday, as inspection officer of the navy yard.

Bremerton's business section will be afforded the protection of the salt water mains of the navy yard in fighting fire, if the recommendations of Rear Admiral V. L. Cottman, U. S. N., commandant of the navy yard, are approved by the navy department. This will give Bremerton a fire protection system not surpassed by any other city of the Northwest, with volume and pressure sufficient to successfully combat any blaze.

The commandant, in a communication to the city council Oct. 9, expressed a willingness to recommend that the city be allowed to connect with the salt water mains, provided the city will be willing to comply with certain rules and regulations which the navy department will exact. The commandant was notified of the city's willingness to comply.

The "Olympian" leaves Seattle 10:15 a. m. every day—
C. M. & P. S. Ry.

Word from the Mare Island navy yard has it that the cruiser Albany, now in Asiatic waters, will go to Mare Island early next year, for a complete overhauling. The Albany has heretofore made her home port at the Bremerton yard.

On Monday, October 30, the working hours of the navy yard were changed to conform with the short winter days. The workmen are allowed only a half hour at noon, and the yard shuts down at 4:30 every evening, instead of 5 o'clock. This schedule will remain in effect until about the middle of February.

NEWS FROM THE PHILADELPHIA.

Sixty men were enlisted between Oct. 1st and 27th.

The football team of the Philadelphia defeated the U. S. S. Pennsylvania with a score of 20 to 0, and the Mucklucks of Seattle, with a score of 131 to 0.

Thirty G. C. M. prisoners are expected from the Navy Yard, Mare Island, Cal., via the U. S. S. Oregon, for confinement on the Nipsic.

Paymaster R. B. Lupton reported aboard for duty as the relief of Paymaster T. J. Bright, U. S. N., ordered to the Asiatic station.

Mate W. O. Lamb will, upon re-enlistment Nov. 10, 1911, be transferred to the U. S. S. Pensacola for duty.

Paymaster John M. Hancock, U. S. N., is coaching the Philadelphia football team and is also acting in the capacity of captain.

The Phila's football team will play the following games during November:

Nov. 4—University of Puget Sound, at Tacoma.

Nov. 11—Multnomah Club, at Portland.

Nov. 14—Vancouver Barracks, at Vancouver, Wash.

Nov. 19—Rainier Valley Athletic Club, at Seattle.

C. F. Marquardt, Yeo. 1cl. formerly of the Pennsylvania, has been confined to the sick bay, suffering with blood poison in his left foot.

The Philadelphia prides itself in having in Neil Roy, one of the best and most conscientious commissary stewards in the service. Roy came to the Philadelphia from the Pennsylvania.

SPORTS

The Philly team tasted defeat at the hand of the Wenatchee team, one of the fastest teams in the Northwest, at Wenatchee—26-0. This is the only beating that the Philly team has received to date and let's hope that its her last. But a few days later she took revenge on the light, but game, Mucklucks of Seattle, running up and down the field until she had a total of 131 points. The Philly team outweighed the Hardlucks 20 pounds, but the Haplucks were game although they could do nothing against the strong team they were playing at the time mentioned. The Philly used the forward pass and got away with it nine out of every ten attempts. But as the game was never in doubt, a little kicking for field goals would have been to the liking of all hands also for the betterment of the team, but they failed to try for any field goals, so the game ended with the Philly headed for another touchdown.

The Bremerton crack baseball team lost to the Seattle professionals 2-0. Although Gordon pitched a good game his team mates failed to hit the Seatle twirlers to advantage, therefore the Bremerton squad was whitewashed.

For the second consecutive year the Philadelphia Athletics won the highest honors in baseball, beating the "invincibles" known in all departments of the game. It was undoubtedly the greatest world's series ever staged, as the first five games played were anybodys game, neither side scoring over 4 runs. But the great Mathewson and the famous Rube Marquard proved to be easy marks for the hard hitting Athletics, although they did not hit either very hard. The Giants failed to show that speed for which they were noted, and the Athletics romped away with the final game at Philadelphia, 13-2. They made as many runs in the last game as the Muggsyites accumulated in six games. The teams were evenly matched before the series, to most of the scribes, but now the tale has been transferred. Well, let New York take care of

The "Milwaukee" Is the New Steel Trail.

The Pennsy Football Squad

**Check Your Baggage from Bremerton direct—
Via the Milwaukee.**

itself as both teams can't be winners and as the saying goes, the best team won the title of "The World's Champions, 1912."

On Saturday, October 4th, our football team journeyed to Fort Warden, only to be defeated by the soldier team of that place, 59-0. It was our first game of the season and Captain Sloane's bunch of pig skin artists did well to hold the strong fort team to 59 points. The result of the game lies in the fact that the soldiers used the on-side kick and the forward pass quite frequently and managed to get away with it nearly every time. But—

Later in the month we gave the Phillies the game of their career, although we lost 20-0. The game was enlivened with many sensational plays on both sides. Before the game all hands were figuring how many hundred points the Philly aggregation would roll up against us, but immediately after the game got under way the tune swayed. The game opened with Philly receiving the ball and after many failures at the forward pass she returned the ball to us. We managed to get through with a couple of passes for gains but lost the ball to the Philly team on a fumble. After the Philly team saw that it was useless to try and hold us from going through her line and breaking up her play in the backfield before the quarter could pass the ball, the strange part of it was that she still used the same line of defense. After ten minutes of play the first period ended with the score standing 2-0 in favor of the Philly bunch, as she scored a safety. In the second period we managed to hold our own and then some—for Captain Sloane was playing the game of his life, breaking up her team work and getting their goats on the side. He had the Phillies all going sideways. Although we were unable to cross the Phillie's line we defended ours to perfection and the second period ended with the score reading 2-0. The features of the first half was the all-around playing of our peerless leader, Captain Sloane, and the snappy play of Storman, our lightning end. During the intermission the Philly team was somewhat worried as they had failed to cross our line for a touchdown in the first half of the game. Our team was considerably fagged for they had to exert themselves to the limit to hold the opposing team safe. The third quarter opened with a rush and after a few minutes of play it was seen that the strain was telling on us and the Phillies planted the ball safely between our goal for the first touchdown of the game—the goal was kicked and the score stood, at the end of the third period, 8-0. All Philly. The last period saw our last stand; we were fighting to hold the score down—Quarterback Sloane was doing great work and had the rest of the team doing the same—but the Philly backfield began to let itself be known and before many minutes of play she had crossed our line for the second touchdown of the game. On the try for the goal the ball sailed clean on one of the prettiest kicks ever seen on the local grounds. This made the score look like 14-0. We had the goose egg, or whatever you want to call it. The Philadelphia backfield was the whole team in this game, for her line was weak—time and again our ends broke up their plays in the backfield before the quarter could pass the ball. The backs were wondering how they were being copped in the act eight out of ten times. But—that but again—their backs were our downfall as they managed to score again after several attempts at the forward pass, a few of which succeeded, and to make things look right (for the Phillie crowd) the ball went over our goal on the kick and the score was advanced six points, making a total of twenty. That was the last score of the game and at 20-0 the final happenings read. The features of the second half were the playing of Sloane, then more Sloane, and the great offensive work of the Phillie's backs, as it was the Philly backs that beat us in that memorable game.

On October 15th we again put on our traveling togs and when the baggage was unloaded and we looked around for the town we found, after much searching for an inhabitant, that we were in the noble town or city of Renton. Did you get that? Renton! Well, how they got a team out that place is hard to say, but they had one just the same. After some rough playing (we were supposed to get beat, so the Renton bugs thought) in which we were penalized for being on sides, off sides, gaining or almost anything, we finally managed to put the ball over the line for a touchdown. Like the town, we will make the score small; for after the battle it was found that Sloane and his Pennsy tribe had triumphed to the tune of 5-0, as we had failed to kick the goal on the try. Good Bye,

Renton, till we meet again, then—we'll bring our best along to the Navy Yard gridiron. Let's see what you can do off your home pasture.

We transferred temporarily, 456 men to the U. S. S. Oregon.

From the U. S. S. St. Louis

The following ravings from the St. Louis, arrived in our last Aero mail:

Wanted:—One Boatswain's mate, a General Storekeeper, and 8 ship keepers, who will carry stores aboard during the day and stand watches at night. Apply in person to Skipper Fosnaugh, dog house, Bridge deck, U. S. S. St. Louis.

There is an unofficial rumor afloat to the effect that the St. Louis will leave Nov. 1st for San Francisco.

"Admiral" Kimball of the steamer Fleet has been seen with his private vessels in these waters lately. All good mariners are warned to be on the lookout for him.

One of our society members was seen moping about the deck the other day with a face as long as a payday liberty list, and on being questioned as to the cause of his gloom, burst forth with this mournful ditty:

> "Mary had a little waist
> She laced it smaller still;
> A stone o'er Mary has been placed,
> Out on the silent hill.
> "And on that stone these words are writ:
> 'Oh, let us hope she's gone,
> Where Angels never care a bit,
> About what they have on.' "

I have actually seen: A cigar box, a square dance, a brick walk and a whisky punch.—Ike Boyle.

F. Brady; W. T., who was discharged early in October re-enlisted on the ship, took his thirty days and reported on the U. S. S. Franklin.

**Check Your Baggage from Bremerton direct—
Via the Milwaukee.**

U. S. S. GOLDSBOROUGH NOTES.

Our able bodied mess cook, B. Magee, O. S., will challenge any mess cook for lightning and speedy work. He claims he is the only mess cook in existence, who allows no grass to grow under his feet. Away, rapid transit.

Mr. Mutt, our Torpedo Expert, otherwise known as Kid Batemout, will meet any gunner's mate at slinging oil or vaseline.

The U. S. S. Goldsborough is thinking of starting a menagerie. We already have a mule, a cat and a little snowbird. Who said cats? Me-ow. Ask Martin Beuelow.

Kid Feese, the pride of the flotilla, is willing to meet any man in his class at 138 pounds, ringside. Consult his manager, Mr. Perez.

Master Singleton, the heart-breaker of the Goldsborough, is very much broken up over losing his home in Bremerton. But he is not slow, by no means, and it is a good gamble he will win another within the week.

Mr. Minser, otherwise known as little Midget, the belle of the Pacific flotilla, is willing to meet any so-called beauty at a beauty contest.

A reward of $100 cash is offered to any man in the Pacific fleet who can give a sure cure for sleeping meningitis. Apply to McGrew, sometimes called Feather, U. S. S. Goldsborough.

SHORT TIMERS FOR NOVEMBER.

Date	Name	Rate	U. S. S.
3	Penny, L. C.	S. F. 2cl	Pennsylvania
3	Williams, N. T.	M. M. 1cl	Oregon
6	Harry, G. F.	C. P.	Oregon
8	Stone, G. S.	Seaman	Pennsylvania
11	Lacy, J. C.	W. T.	Oregon
12	Faraday, C. F.	Boats'n M. 2cl	Oregon
13	Ross, J. C.	G. M. 1cl	Oregon
17	Lemming, B. H.	F. 1cl.	Oregon
19	O'Donnell, C. J.	W. T.	Oregon
20	Bullen, G. L.	E. 1cl.	Oregon
23	Chamberlain, R. R.	M. A. A. 3cl.	Pennsylvania
26	Schillo B.	Seaman	Pennsylvania
27	Ross, W. A.	Seaman	Oregon
29	Jolidan	G. M. 3cl.	Pennsylvania
29	Bartko, A. M.	C. P.	Oregon

In California

Armored Cruiser Sailor:— "Gee! I wish I was a Battle-ship sailor.

BULL DOG GROWLS
FROM THE U. S. S. OREGON

D AWSON Says that he doesn't object to having the other steam boat men of the fleet call him a "Bull Dog" sailor. But the title of "Pup" as applied to his steamer does rather get his nanny.

It didn't take our fellows long to get those Oregon cap ribbons sewed on, did it?

Miller says this life is awful. On the Pennsy they wouldn't let him enjoy his meals on mess 29, with their yarn on what happened in the galley, and now—well the Oregon is not the easiest of sea boats.

Jimmie Kinkaid says he'll land that soft snap yet.

It is rumored that this ship is to take a draft of G. C. M. prisoners to the Nipsic. Many of our men are wondering where we are going to put them.

Oh you bag inspection!

"Take me back to my Pennsylvania Home," or "Why did I want to be a Battleship Sailor?" Sung with great success by the ex-U. S. S. Pennsylvania's Amusement Co.'s chorus girls.

All day long and far into the night the sound of hammer and saw rang. At last it was finished. The ordinary seaman who was piloting visitors about the ship in Frisco stopped in front of the structure and pointed to it with pride. "Oh, what is it?" cried they in chorus as they viewed its padded interior, "a cold storage plant?"

"Nay," answered the youthful tar, "that's where we keep the married men since we left Bremerton."

Guess some of our deck force will be sure enough seamen when we hit Bremerton again.

Well, anyhow fellows, we have it on the rest of the fleet. We are the only battleship sailors on the station.

A "Milwaukee" Ticket Office right In Bremerton.

Naval Y. M. C. A. Notes.

"All is quiet along the Potomac." The saying holds true at the Association building. The men of the Pennsylania who were transferred to the Oregon are greatly missed.

Word which came from other branches of the Navy Y. M. C. A. during the past month indicates the growing interest of the service in Association activities.

Brooklyn and Norfolk are pushing their Fall educational work and many men are taking advantage of the courses of study offered. Vallejo and San Francisco report active times while the fleet was in.

The illustrated lecture on the Panama Canal by Edwin R. Gobrecht of Boone, Iowa, on October 14th was very interestng and instructive.

As a result of the recent membership campaign 32 men from the U. S. S. Pennsylvania joined the Association. Thanks are due to all who had a part in boosting the interest of the Association. Membership is a growth. Let present members keep the question alive and growth will come.

Announcement is made at this time of the Union Revival services to be conductd by Rev. and Mrs Wm. Parks at the Coliseum Rink commen'ing November 8th,

---

Cold weather is almost upon us and still we tarry in the Navy Yard. What, with putting other ships in commission, filling their holds with stores and their bunkers with coal, and the large amount of work to be done on our own old Pennsy, all hands are kept exceedingly busy and it is a safe bet that no one will be sorry to leave.

In Norfolk, the ship's papers are considerably agitated over the refusal of the Retail Merchants Association to endorse them as advertising mediums. It would almost seem as though the Norfolk merchants didn't want the Bluejackets' patronage. If, however, the men were denied liberty in Norfolk, this same association would undoubtedly lost no time in finding out why, and doing their utmost to relieve the situation.

Yes, we'll all be glad when we get where a bunch of Navy Yard workmen can not come in and rub the greese off their dungarees on our paint-work and spit tobacco juice all over our deck.

Deal with "Van" and get a square deal.

STRAY SHOTS

We are very sorry to state that our friend Knight has contracted a severe cold, due to losing his curly locks. Now it would be very generous if his shipmates would contribute a few pesos and buy him a wig. We believe it woudl be highly appreciated by the afflicted.

Did you ever notice the smile on the bumboat's face when he learns that hash, sharko or free lunch is on the menu?

Blondie says she is an awful sweet girl, but it takes the Mazuma to go to Seattle every Saturday. Better get a book, Blondie.

Speaking about averaged sized men—throw Snookums Ryan and Fat Austin in a sausage machine and divide by two.

On the square, don't you miss the chorus girls?

Do you like your job honey? Oh, you St. Louis working party!

Who was it who slept in a rain barrel in the rear of the Rainier Grand? Oh you G. S. K. mystery!

"Cussin' the other feller is like puttin' paint on the bottom of the overhead—you'll always get mussed yourself."—Salty.

The man who used to cuss the canteen yeoman is beginning to think he wasn't such a bad plug after all. "Gimme the butt.'

We sure miss that red knob of Brady's.

We'll all testify to the fact that there is some class to "Bugs" as a cook. "Bugs" says "dogs is dogs, but hot dogs is grub." Hot dogs is right.

The "Columbian" leaves Seattle 7:15 p. m. every day— via The Milwaukee.

"When we rounded the Horn in '98"

Take your homeward bounder on the Best Road—The
Milwaukee.

Now which would you rather do, take a bath in icy water and kill an hour changing clothes, or stay on the job in dry clothes without the bath? Ask the lad who fell (?) off the propeller one cold October morning when the Pennsy came in dry dock.

Those socialistic fanatics will raise the red flag in the print shop yet, if they don't let up on that line of talk to the printer.

On the square fellows, wouldn't some of those awful yarns of Sefton's come in handy these cold mornings—before they turn the steam on?

Webster says a short-timer is a man who has less than six months to serve in the navy. Seems like a lot of these 1912 men are doing a lot of unauthorized hollering now days.

Look out there, Pin Head, that terrible head hunter from South Africa will catch you one of these days.

Stinson says the ignorance of some of these sailors is appaling. The other day he got a chit for a plug of ship's, an accordion and a box of dog biscuit.

Butter, butter, who's got the butter? Ask any man on mess six.

Ordinary seamen showing visitors about the ship. "Now you would think from these fellow's antics that they had just been transferred from the funny house, but such is not the case. That wild eyed maniacal looking fellow you see there at the telephone is George Heller. He is getting the returns from the World's championship games."

When the Pennsy leaves the yard, Bremerton society may recover, but it will never look the same.

In the old Navy they used to unchain the dogs of war; now they uncan them.—Jayhawker.

Fast women and slow horses have put many a man to the bad. How about it, Wiggles?

HELP WANTED.

Telephone girls wanted for new telephone system. Apply to Mr. Mack, 125 Berth Deck Ave., near hospital.

Two refined young ladies to learn nursing. See Dr. Hughes, General Hospital.

Young man wanted to clerk in general store. Must be willing to work long hours and Sundays. Will be paid $21 a month to start, with room and board. Apply to manager, Mr. Mapps.

Two young lady stenographers in print shop; must have great speed and accuracy to enable them to take the ravings of the society editor.

Two messengers wanted. Call on Mr. Heller, Penn. Bldg., 3rd floor.

Wanted—Every one to know that Sea-Going socks are the real dope. Ask the printer.

COMEDY.

And now we will be entertained, gentlemen and sailors, by that engaging pair of commedians, Mr. Giles and Mr. Woods:

Giles—Give me a two-cent stamp.

Woods—Cancelled or uncancelled?

Giles—Either kind. Shall I put it on myself?

Woods—No, you hay shaker, put it on the letter. (There's where you laugh.)

Giles—What made you put your girl's picture in your watch?

Woods—Because I think she will love me in time. (Giles promptly faints). While Giles is coming out of the dope, Woods springs this one on an innocent and nususpecting audience:

"We are very glod to remain in Bremerton for the climate is considered very healthy in the winter time. Only one man died here in the last ten years and he was a doctor. He died of starvation.

Giles (who has recovered)—What time is it?

Woods—My watch is out of order.

Giles—What's the matter with it?

Woods—I got bed bugs in it.

Giles—How did they get in there?

Woods—They crawled in between the ticks, you mutt! Giles does a flip flop and then goes through the audience selling their latest book entitled, "The Mystery of Speedy Rictor, or Who Threw the Deck Swab in His Morning Coffee." (Exit the villains.)

THE HOME OF THE

REGAL SHOE

IN SEATTLE

OPPOSITE

HOTEL

SAVOY

1211 SECOND AVE.

WHAT ARE YOU WORTH?

Have you any special Ability?
What can you do?
How well can you do it?
How much are you worth from Your Neck up?
Can you deliver the goods that will get you the money.

That is the Line of talk that is handed out to the candidate for advancement.

We will teach you the ins and outs of any trade or profession that you choose to follow.

If you knew the why as well as the how, you wouldn't have to ask for more pay: You would just naturally get it.

Dont wait until tomorrow to get started
Call around TODAY and find out all about it.

INTERNATIONAL CORRESPONDENCE SCHOOL
SCRANTON, PA.

J Fisher,
Representative

806 Front St.

CPSIA information can be obtained
at www.ICGtesting.com
Printed in the USA
LVHW022151211218
601373LV00015B/500/P

9 781332 874804